The Little Book
of Olympic Inspiration

Trade Life
P.O. Box 55325
Tulsa, OK 74155

The Little Book of Olympic Inspiration
ISBN 0-88144-197-X
Copyright © 1996 by Trade Life
P.O. Box 55325
Tulsa, Oklahoma 74155

Manuscript prepared by W. B. Freeman Concepts, Tulsa, Oklahoma

Introduction

*W*hat does it take to win a medal in the Olympics? Certainly athletic ability is required, but physical perfection is not. Participating athletes have included those who were partially paralyzed, had withered limbs, or were contending with serious illnesses. They have been young, old, short, tall, male, female, and have represented every major ethnic group in the world.

Becoming a medalist does not require a long series of previous victories. Many world-class athletes have failed to achieve medals, while virtual "unknowns," to the surprise of many, have been elevated to instant fame.

Perhaps the driving force in every Olympic athlete is a deep desire to do their best — to push themselves one step beyond their last achievement.

A "will to win" has kept them focused through years of disciplined training in order to accomplish their dreams.

Such a "will" is not limited to the Olympics or to sports alone. The Spirit of the Olympics resonates in each of us, in every area of our lives. As we watch the events, each victory becomes our encouragement; we too can overcome every obstacle to reach our dreams. To strive for "the gold" is not only an Olympic ideal; it is the very substance of living!■

The Little Book
of Olympic Inspiration

Encouragement and Motivation
Taken from the Glory
of Olympic Achievement

The Little Book of Olympic Inspiration

2000—Sydney
1992—Barcelona
1984—Los Angeles
1976—Montreal
1968—Mexico City
1960—Rome
1952—Helsinki
1936—Berlin
1928—Amsterdam
1920—Antwerp
1908—London
1904—St. Louis
1896—Athens

1996—Atlanta
1988—Seoul
1980—Moscow
1972—Munich
1964—Tokyo
1956—Melbourne
1948—London
1932—Los Angeles
1924—Paris
1912—Stockholm
1906—Athens
1900—Paris

Atlanta Wins!

Most observers didn't think Atlanta had a chance of hosting the 1996 Olympics. Athens was by far the emotionally favored site. But Billy Payne, attorney and former University of Georgia football player, disagreed. He organized the Atlanta Committee for the Olympic Games. In April 1988, after beating 13 other American cities for the right to bid, Payne and Julia Emmons organized a series of road races designed to attract the attention of the International Olympic Committee. At the final race, the IOC delegates were escorted to the race on Atlanta's mass-transit train, where they were met by over 7,500 runners and spectators who spontaneously began chanting, "We want the Games!" Such overwhelming public support was impressive. On September 18, 1990, the IOC awarded the Games of the XXVI Olympiad to Atlanta. The citizens of Atlanta had won their own Olympic contest!

The Olympic Oath

"We swear that we will take part in the Olympic Games in fair competition, respecting the regulations which govern them and with the desire to participate in the true spirit of sportsmanship for the honour of our country and for the glory of sport."

— Administered to competitors
at the opening ceremonies

The First Marathon

"Rejoice! We conquer!"

The last words of Pheidippides, the first "marathoner," who died from exhaustion after running twenty-five miles from the plains of Marathon to Athens, relaying the news of the Greek victory over the Persians in 490 B.C.

The Ancient Games

The first recorded event of the Ancient Olympics was a 200-yard foot race in 776 B.C. Thereafter, the Greeks began recording time by the four-year intervals between each Olympiad.

The foot race was the only event until the 14th Olympiad, when a second foot race of two lengths of the stadium, about 400 yards, was added. Over the years, discus, spear throwing, long jumping, wrestling, and boxing were gradually added.

Olympic contestants had to be free Greek sons of free Greek parents. They tested and trained rigorously and only the best were allowed to compete. For the final month of their training, the athletes were under the strict supervision of the Hellanodicae, the official judges of the Games, who were strict taskmasters. Any athlete who broke a rule would be beaten.

The early Games were part of the religious rites of the ancient Greeks, so athletes were treated as if they were godlike. However, the religious significance of the Games was lost with the rise of the Roman empire, instead they became a pagan carnival. Athletes began demanding money, and corruption eventually led Roman Emperor Theodosius to ban the Games in 394 A.D. Eventually the Olympic temples fell into disuse and were subsequently destroyed by earthquakes and floods. The Ancient Greek Olympic tradition became a memory of the past.■

Amateur Ideal

"*A*mateur sport is a delicate and fragile thing. It is an enlargement of life but it must be pure and honest or it is nothing at all."

— Avery Brundage, President
International Olympic Committee
1952-1972

OLYMPIC FACT:

In ancient Greece, all fighting between Greek villages and states was suspended for three months before the Games.

Ancient Events

*O*ne of the most vicious wrestling events in the ancient Games was the "pancratium" — which permitted every move except biting and gouging. A good strangle-hold was considered a necessary skill in this event. Fatalities were not uncommon. The prize for this effort and risk of life?...A sprig of olive.

OLYMPIC FACT:

Women were barred
from the Ancient
Olympic games until the
128th Olympiad, when a
girl won a chariot race.

Rebirth of the Modern Olympics

*T*he French schools, in the late 1800s had an almost-exclusively intellectual program. Their pupils had no play areas and received little physical training. As a result, France was often prevailed upon in battle by countries with physically stronger soldiers.

Baron Pierre de Coubertin, sought a remedy for this "critical weakness." He began to encourage proficiency in sport and athletic training as a means of furthering the nation's political prowess. Eventually his efforts evolved into the revival of the Olympic Games. He formed a committee to organize the event in November 1894. His efforts were rewarded when the first Olympiad in 14 centuries was held in Athens two years later.

Olympic Resurrection

*T*he first modern international Olympic Games began on Easter Sunday, April 5, 1896. The sound of trumpets was all that announced the arrival of the competitors. Only 311 athletes from 13 countries attended the Games. Greece had the majority of athletes—230 in all. The United States was represented by 14. The program of events included nine sports and 43 events, two of them held for the first time: the marathon race and the discus throw.

Endurance and Determination

*L*asse Virén, a gangling Finnish policeman with a wispy beard, achieved a rare and unexpected double victory on the track in the 1972 Games. He won both the 5,000-meter and 10,000-meter events. Moreover, this was the first Games in which heats were required for the longer distances.

In the final of the 10,000-meter race Virén stayed with the leading group of runners during the opening laps of the race. Just before the halfway point, a runner from Tunisia fell in front of him causing Virén to go down also. Remarkably, he got up and shook off the jarring effects of the fall. Quickly he regained his pace. In the final thrust across the last 600 meters he passed runners from Spain and Belgium to cross the finish line first, besting the world record by one second!

The following day Virén was required to run a qualifying race for the 5,000-meter final. This event had a vastly experienced field, and the weight of conjecture at the time was that one of the "fresh athletes" would win — *not* someone who had endured the strain of a 10,000-meter race. But qualify he did!

When the final race began, Virén stayed with the pack, moving up when a United States runner chose to break. With only four laps remaining, several internationally renowned runners began to make their move — so did Viren! By the time he reached the final straight he was unchallenged! Finns joyously waved their flags as he crossed the line. He was proclaimed a national hero for both the physical and mental stamina he had exhibited when few had faith he could win *two* long-distance medals.■

The Purpose of the Olympics

*T*he International Olympic Committee has defined the following as the true purpose for Olympic competition:

- To draw the world's attention to the fact that physical training and competitive sports develop the health, strength and character of young people.

- To teach the principles of loyal and sporting friendship, which should apply in other spheres of life as well.

- To stimulate the fine arts.

- To put emphasis on sports as games and distractions rather than as commercial business, and to show that the devotion applied to sports is an end in itself, not a means toward material gain.

The Lighting of the Flame

*E*very four years a "priestess" lights an Olympic flame from the light of the sun, enters the stadium in Olympia, and hands the torch to a priestly "king" of the new Olympiad. He then passes the torch to the leader of a team of runners, who usher it out of the stadium to a grove dedicated to Baron de Coubertin, the father of the modern Olympic Games. There an urn is lit on a modern altar, where it burns for the entire duration of the Games.

Another torch, lit from the urn on the altar, is carried by relay until the Olympic flame has reached a temporary home, wherever in the world the Games are about to take place. The lighting of the Olympic flame is considered the highlight of the opening-ceremony festivities.

Back in the Race

After winning a gold medal at the Pan-American Games as part of the 100-meter relay team, track star Valerie Brisco married a college track teammate, Alvin Hooks (then a wide receiver with the Philadelphia Eagles). They had a son the following year. Brisco-Hooks was 40 pounds overweight and had no plans to return to running when her husband challenged her — why not an Olympic medal? Brisco-Hooks took the challenge and embarked on a rigorous training program to get back into shape.

Part of Valerie's determination came from a personal tragedy. Ten years earlier, her brother Robert had been killed from a stray bullet while working out on a track near their home in Los Angeles. She would run in his honor.

She won big at the 1984 Olympics, not one but *three gold medals* — the 200-meter, 400-meter, and 100-meter relay. She is the only athlete to have won both the 200 and 400 in the same Olympics.

Also in 1984, she became the first American woman to break the 50-second mark in the 400 event, with a time of 49.83 seconds. She set a world indoor record of 52.99 in the 400 in 1985, and in 1986 she became the national champion in the 400-meter event.■

The Olympic Flag

*T*he Olympic flag, designed by Baron de Coubertin, was first unfurled at the opening of the 1920 Games. The five interlocking and multicolored circles symbolize the five great land masses as the Baron saw them: Europe, Asia, Africa, Australia, and North and South America. At least one of the colors used for the circles appears in every national flag.

OLYMPIC FACT:

The first time a victory stand was used in the Olympic Games was in Los Angeles in 1932. The awards ceremony was accompanied by the playing of the victors' national anthem and the unfurling of the national flag.

Olympic Village

*I*n order to accomplish its goal of providing low-cost housing for 1,500 athletes from 34 nations, the Olympic Committee for the 1932 Los Angeles Games discussed the creation of an Olympic Village, where all athletes might live in a community atmosphere.

Located on a hilltop only ten minutes from the Olympic stadium, the village consisted of two-room, Mexican-ranch-style cottages built on 250 landscaped acres. The village had a variety of dining rooms to accommodate each athlete's preference in food. It also contained a hospitality house, hospital, fire department, and recreation area.

The village, however, was only for the use of male athletes. Female athletes were housed exclusively at the spacious Chapman Park Hotel.

Photo Finish!

*T*he 1932 Games was the first time an electric photo-timing device was introduced for races. Prior races had been hand-timed only. In 1932, hand-timing was still considered the "official time," so the electric system served as a backup. Very early in the Games, however, the photo-timing device helped judges determine the winner in the 100-meter dash, in which two runners from the United States finished only inches apart.

OLYMPIC FACT:

In the early days of the modern Olympic movement, athletes had a casual approach to training. At one time, it was possible to train only three days a week and still achieve the skill level necessary to compete at the Games. In fact, it was considered "ungentlemanly" to push the body too hard.

The Agony of Victory

"It was a new kind of agony for me. My head was exploding, my stomach ripping and even the tips of my fingers ached. The only thing I could think was, 'If I live, I will never run again!'"

—Tom Courtney, Two Gold Medals
1956 Melbourne Games

A Winning Streak

*E*velyn Ashford had one of the longest and most successful careers of any sprinter in history. She was a member of five U.S. Olympic teams and won a total of nine medals, four of them gold.

"When I caught my first glimpse of the gold medal while I waited on the victory stand, I was emotionally overcome. I couldn't believe it was over. I couldn't stop crying."

— Evelyn Ashford, Gold Medalist
1984 Los Angeles Games

Opening Ceremonies in Ancient Greece

*T*he opening processional of the ancient Greek Games took two days and covered a 34-mile sacred route from Elis to Olympia. Prior to embarking, the athletes were told by the judges:

> If you have practiced hard for Olympia, and if you have not been lazy, or done anything dishonorable, then go forward with confidence. But if any of you have not trained yourselves this way, then leave us and go where you choose.

Judges' Oath

*A*fter the athletes had given their oath, the judges swore to take no bribes, to make their decisions fairly, and to keep secret the reasons for their judgments.

Olympic Prizes 1896

*D*uring the first Olympic Games of the modern era, only the first and second place finishers in each event received prizes: the first, a diploma, a silver medal, and a crown of olive branches; the second, a diploma, a bronze medal, and a crown of laurel.

All competitors in the Games received a commemorative medal. King George I of Greece awarded all prizes on the last day of the Games.

A Horse and Cart

*F*ollowing the 1896 Games, King George asked Spiridon Loues, the winner of the marathon, what he would like as a gift. Loues replied he would like a horse and cart so he could carry fresh water more conveniently from his village to Athens, a distance of about seven kilometers.

Loues' village had clear fresh water, which Athens badly needed. He was in the habit of making two daily trips on a mule loaded with two barrels of water. Every morning and evening Loues would run the seven kilometers beside the mule, deliver his water, then ride the mule home. Little did he realize he was creating a "twice-a-day" training method which is now used almost universally by world-class marathon runners.

Winning Cousins

*P*aul Costello and his cousin, John B. Kelly, won the double-sculls event in back-to-back Olympics of 1920 and 1924. Costello then went on to win the event a third time, with Charles McIlvaine as his partner, making him the first rower to win three consecutive Olympic gold medals in the same event.

No Broken Necks

*A*fter Dick Fosbury won the 1968 Olympic gold medal in the high jump, the U.S. Coach, Payton Jordan, said:

> "Kids imitate champions. If they try to imitate Fosbury, he'll wipe out an entire generation of high jumpers because they all will have broken necks."

Twelve years later, 13 of the 16 finalists in the Olympic high jump were using the "Fosbury flop" — in which the jumper goes over the bar headfirst and backward — there were no broken necks.

From Scars to Honors

When he was only six years old, Glenn Cunningham and his older brother Floyd were starting a fire in the schoolhouse stove one cold February morning, a routine chore for them. The kerosene container, however, had accidently been filled with gasoline on this particular morning. As the boys lit the fire, the stove exploded. Floyd was killed and Glenn's legs were so badly burned his physicians feared he would never walk again.

After several weeks in bed, Glenn was finally able to walk with crutches. Later he discovered, "It hurt like thunder to walk, but it didn't hurt at all when I ran." So for the next five or six years, all he did was run.

Because of circulation problems caused by his accident, Cunningham needed at least an hour of preparation for each run.

After massaging his legs, he would undergo a strenuous routine of warm-up exercises.

A miler in high school, he continued with track events at the University of Kansas. His first Olympic Games were in 1932, where he finished fourth in the 1,500-meter race. In 1933, after setting a world record of 4:06.7 for the mile, he was given the prized Sullivan Award for becoming America's most outstanding amateur athlete. In the 1936 Games, he came from behind and received a silver medal.

Cunningham later earned a doctoral degree from New York University. After working at Cornell College and serving in the Navy, he and his wife opened the Glenn Cunningham Youth Ranch in Kansas, where they helped to rear some 10,000 underprivileged children.■

Glory in Doing One's Best

"In the dust of defeat as well as in the laurels of victory there is a glory to be found if one has done his best."

— Eric Liddell, 1924 Paris Games
Gold Medal Runner

Secret Strategy

"*I* let my feet spend as little time on the ground as possible. From the air, fast down, and from the ground, fast up. My foot is only a fraction of the time on the track."

— Jesse Owens, Runner
4 gold medals, 1936 Berlin Games

Springing Back!

*A*lthough she was considered "old" in diving circles, Micki King was a favorite going into the 1968 Olympics. In her ninth dive she hit the board and broke her left forearm. Although she went on to perform her tenth and final dive with a broken arm, she could not overcome the penalty from her ninth dive and ended in fourth place.

Four years later, however, she received her coveted gold medal. After taking the lead with her eighth dive, she finished the competition with the same reverse 1-1/2 somersault she was performing when she broke her arm.

Sports Longevity

"I've been diving longer than the girl who came in second has lived!"

— Micki King, 1972 Munich Games
Gold Medal, Diving

OLYMPIC FACT:

Alice Coachman was the first black woman to win an Olympic gold medal — in the high jump — and was the only American woman to win a track and field event at the 1948 Olympics.

Wrestler Extraordinaire

*P*erhaps the greatest Olympic star of all time was Milo of Corton, who competed in the sixth century B.C. and won the wrestling crown at Olympia six times. He remained undefeated in every match he entered. For generations the Greeks wrote and sang of his feats.

Milo was said to have developed his great strength by carrying a calf on his shoulders every day of its life until it was a full-grown bull.

He often demonstrated his strength to his admirers with an entire repertoire of stunts. In one, he would hold a pomegranate so firmly that no one could force open his fingers, yet so controlled was his grip he never damaged the fruit. In another stunt, he stood barefoot on an oiled disk and dared anyone to push or rush him off. No one could budge him.

Going the Distance

A true champion has what it takes to go the extra distance, even if his race is finished. That's the lesson Abel Kiviat demonstrated when he ran in the 1912 Olympic trials. As he crossed the finish line of the 1,500-meter race, setting a world record that lasted many years, several judges rushed out crying to him, "Go for the mile! Go for the mile!" Abel couldn't understand what they meant since the mile is more than 120 yards further than 1,500 meters. He took nearly 20 seconds to run the extra distance since he had begun to slow down after crossing the finish line of his race. Even so, he tied the current world record for the mile!

Abel won gold and silver medals in the 1912 Stockholm Olympics.

Challenged to Run

"*I* really started running while chasing after my brother. We used to get up every morning and milk the cows by hand. In the winter we took them to a pasture that was about two miles from our house. On the way home my brother would give me about a 100-yard head start, and we'd race back home to catch the school bus at a quarter to seven. I'd do anything to keep him from catching me, but since he was four years older than I, he would always catch me about 25 or 30 yards from the house. But one day he didn't catch me — so he stopped giving me a lead."

— Fred Newhouse, 1976 Montreal Games
Gold and Silver Medalist

Even the Unlikely

*F*rom his childhood, Lanny Bassham had a strong desire to be an athlete, but he was short and clumsy. Intrigued by the Olympics, he read about one event where size, weight, and large-muscle skills were not essential. He won silver (1972) and gold (1976) medals as a marxman for small-bore rifle shooting.

All-Around Athlete

*O*ne of the greatest all-around athletes of all time was Rafer Johnson. He finished second in the decathlon at the 1956 Melbourne Games, but that was his last defeat. At a dual meet in 1958, he set a world record of 8,302 points.

In 1959 an automobile accident left him unable to train for more than a year-and-a-half. Nevertheless, Johnson participated in the 1960 Rome Games, where he persevered to win the gold medal.

Johnson was the first black to carry the American flag at the Olympic ceremonies (1960). In 1984, he was selected to light the torch at the opening ceremonies of the Los Angeles Olympics.

The Mind First

"*I* felt in my coaching career that if I would work on their head, their bodies would come along. A lot of coaches work on their bodies and then at the last moment try to do their heads. The thing is if they are working with their heads all the time, and working with head over body, mind over matter, they will have more confidence when they walk up to the block."

— Flip Darr, swimming coach to eight Olympic medalists

Two Attributes

A physician once had this to say about the long-striding track and field star from Finland in the late 1960s, Lasse Virén:

"Lasse has exceptionally good body parts. But they aren't, as you might think, his two legs. They are his heart and head."

Never Give Up

*A*n Olympic victor who perhaps personifies the "Never give up" attitude more than any other was Arrachion of ancient Phigalia. Competing in the pancratium — an intense wrestling-boxing event — Arrachion was being strangled by his opponent. Almost unconscious, he managed to grab his opponent's foot and with a great burst of energy, twist it out of its socket. His rival felt such intense pain he relinquished his hold and raised his hand to the referee, acknowledging defeat. Even as he did, victorious Arrachion gasped his last breath.

Middle-Age Marvel

*R*ay Ewry had been a sickly child who spent a good deal of his youth as an invalid. His physician suggested he take up exercise in order to build his body's strength, which was somewhat of a novel idea at the time. Ray's determination to get well eventually drove him to develop a pair of legs which seemed to be made of steel springs. In college, he specialized in jumping events.

Ray went to his first Games in Paris in 1900 at the late age of 27. He won all the gold medals available in jumping events in both 1900 and 1904. At age 35, he competed in his third and final Olympics, winning gold medals in both jumping events. He retired from athletics after winning ten gold medals, more than any other Olympic athlete. As of 1996 his record remains unbroken.

The Challenge

"*I* enjoyed swimming because I was really racing the stopwatch. That meant I could beat the John Naber of yesterday. My daily progress was my reward, and my perpetual goal was to do a personal best by the end of each season. Every year I wanted to be better than I was the year before, and I would always tell myself that if I were not, I should quit. Fortunately, I did do a little bit better every year, even the year after the Olympics."[1]

— John Naber, Swimmer
4 Gold Medals, 1 Silver Medal
1976 Montreal Games

Every Olympian a Winner

*A*lthough she finished well down the list in the archery competition at the 1984 Games in Los Angeles, Neroli Fairhall of Christchurch, New Zealand, scored a great victory. A paraplegic, Fairhall had been confined to a wheelchair for 15 years because of a motorcycle accident which ended her career as an equestrian. Using the same equipment as the other archers on the line, she was a spirited example of the Olympic dream. From the opening ceremonies, when she wheeled into the Coliseum in her blue New Zealand blazer and white slacks, through the last fireworks of the closing ceremonies, she was a true champion.

All-Around Excellence

*T*he Games were originally based on a concept of Greek philosophy called *areté*, which means excellence in every area of life: physically, intellectually, and morally. Contestants were initially screened by a ten-man panel of judges. A single blot on a young man's character — even some questionable act on the part of his father or mother — would disqualify him as surely as if he had failed a physical test.

Only One Answer

"[An] unforgettable memory from Munich was the Israeli massacre. Everything was so nice in the Village. There we were, athletes from all over the world. We could shake hands, talk to one another through interpreters, and exchange gifts. So I began to think that maybe all that I'd heard about the problems of the world just wasn't true. I thought that maybe there could be peace on earth. Maybe man could find his own solutions, and just maybe sports could lead the way...

"When I found out what happened, I was jolted back into reality. As the Bible tells us, we are of a sinful nature, and getting together for a friendly competition is not going to change that....So, to me, the only answer is God."[2]

— Benjamin Lee Person, Wrestler
Gold Medal, 1972 Munich Games
Silver Medal, 1976 Montreal Games

Determination

*I*f an Olympic medal was awarded for personal determination and ingenuity, it would have to go to Felix Carvajal, an athlete in the 1904 Games. Felix was a Cuban postman who decided that running his daily rounds had prepared him for the Olympic marathon race. Since Cuba had no team, Felix had to personally finance his trip. He did this primarily by running around and around the town square until a crowd gathered. Then he would give a fund-raising speech and accept contributions.

When he finally had enough money to travel to the Games in St. Louis, he resigned his job and set sail for New Orleans. Once ashore, he was met by a gambler and robbed of nearly everything he had. Undeterred, he set out to run from New Orleans to St. Louis. Begging food along the way, he finally arrived in the

Olympic City half-starved. The news of his determination arrived before he did and many fellow athletes rallied to his support. Robbed of his running gear, he cut out the arms and legs of his clothing to accommodate the intense heat and humidity. A fellow athlete loaned him a pair of sneakers for the race, but Felix insisted on running in his postman's boots. His unusual athletic wear was a sight.

Because of the oppressive heat, many of the 31 marathon runners did not even finish the race. But Felix remained undeterred and ran far ahead of the pack. Unfortunately, as he passed an orchard he picked an apple and ate it as he ran. The apple gave him such a stomach cramp he had to sit on a curb to recover while others passed him. Even so, once recovered, Felix came roaring back into the race and finished fourth! To his fellow competitors and observers alike, he had a medal-winning spirit.■

The Victor's Moment

"There is nothing that can compare to the medal ceremony at an Olympic Games. You can never recreate that moment. But the first time you do it and the first time you break a world record, and the first time you stand at the top of the podium with the flag of your country above the others is probably a combination of most of the emotions that you are capable of feeling. There is joy, satisfaction, pride, and a twinge of sadness because you will never quite repeat that again. The race is gone and it is in the history books....You are sad because it was a one time thing and the mold was broken for good. It's a wonderful feeling and that is why we do it."[3]

— David Wilkie, Great Britain
Gold Medalist, 1976 Montreal Games

A Rare Second-Chance Win

*A*t the 1956 Melbourne Games, the Yale rowing crew demonstrated the ability to take full advantage of a second chance. A provision in the sport of rowing allows one losing team a second chance, called a *repechage*, by racing and winning against the other heat losers. Historically no crew had ever lost a qualifying heat and gone on to win a gold medal. The team moved at an incredible rate and won the heat.

Knowing the Yale team had faced three brutal days of all-out effort, the Aussies (with strength still in reserve) were heavily favored to win.

However, driven by the memory of that second chance, Yale hit an amazing 40 strokes a minute pace — five or six strokes more than they had ever achieved before — to win the gold.

Training

"*Y*ou can't just train hard; everybody trains hard. Look around, see how the others train, and train harder than they do."

— Dennis Pursley, Swimming Coach to
U.S. Gold Medalist Mary T. Meagher

Triple

*J*ust a few months before the 1964 Tokyo Games, swimmer Dawn Fraser chipped a neck vertebra in an automobile accident that took the life of her mother. The courageous 27-year-old champion, winner of gold in both the 1956 and 1960 Games, rebounded from her physical injury and grief to swim to gold in Tokyo. She became the first swimmer in Olympic history to win the same event in three successive Games.

The Final Lap

Billy Mills won the first U.S. Olympic gold medal in the 10,000-meter race during the 1964 Tokyo Games. It was so spectacular he was immediately pulled off the track for an interview. Billy was due a "victory lap," but so many runners had yet to finish the final lap officials felt it would be too confusing. Billy left Tokyo feeling a deep disappointment.

Many years later, Billy and his wife Pat were back at the same stadium in Tokyo to participate in a documentary about the 1964 Games. As the crew set up to film his segment, Billy felt oddly compelled to begin a walk-run lap around the track. As the rain poured, he suddenly realized he was taking his long-awaited victory lap. He began to cry, as he neared the stands, when he heard one person clapping for him — Pat. She knew how badly he needed that lap to capstone his victory.

The Opinion that Counted

"I suppose I was the only person who thought I had a chance."

— Billy Mills, Gold Medalist
1964 Tokyo Games

A Dramatic Upset!

*E*veryone has an "off day," but rarely does it impact a career as it did for hurdler "Bones" Dillard. Considered to be the greatest hurdler the world had seen, Bones struck the second hurdle while attempting to qualify for the 1948 Olympic team and didn't even finish the race. For an unexplained reason, he also entered himself in the 100-meter dash. As a hurdler, he wasn't on par with the great 100-meter competitors of his time, but he managed to squeak into third place and won a spot on the U.S. team after all!

At the Games in London, Bones again amazed spectators by barely qualifying in every heat leading to the finals of the 100-meter race. In the final race, he drew the disadvantageous outside lane.

Nobody figured him to be in the race — all eyes were focused on the two favorites, Patton and Ewell. When Ewell crossed the finish line with a lunge, just seconds ahead of Patton, he thought he had won, but his victory smile faded quickly when he realized Bones had beaten him to the line! The world's greatest hurdler, who had failed in his specialty, had achieved a most dramatic upset! ■

Good Sportsmanship

*H*opelessly outclassed in the 10,000-meter run in the 1932 Los Angeles Games, a Japanese runner was nevertheless determined to finish his race. At the point where most runners were already ahead of him by at least a lap, he realized his running position on the inside of the track might cost front runners precious fractions of a second as they had to run around him. So, he moved over and ran the last several laps of his race in the third lane. This allowed the winner of the race to break a 16-year-old Olympic record for the event. The Japanese runner finished by himself, a lonely last, but he was rewarded with tremendous applause for his sportsmanship from an admiring crowd.

The Workout Within

"*A* workout has to be 'within.' There can't be sacrifices. There must be dedication. If workouts are sacrifices, you are missing out. I certainly don't think that a swimmer should say, 'I'm sacrificing!' If they are sacrificing, they are not doing it right. They have to want to do it, because when a swimmer wants to do it, you get great workouts because they are self-motivated."

— Flip Darr, swimming coach
of eight Olympic medalists

Three Minutes

*I*n the 1964 Tokyo Games, American shot-put champion Randy Matson cut loose with a put of 66 feet, 3-1/4 inches, almost two feet better than the previous Olympic record. But Randy scarcely had time to put on his sweater before his teammate, Dallas Long, impatiently tore into the shot-put circle, stepped up to the heaving spot, and let fly with a winning put of 66 feet, 8-1/2 inches.

Matson was an Olympic record-holder for...three minutes.

Grace and Forgiveness

*I*n the 5,000-meter race at the 1932 Games, a Finnish runner was in the lead with an American only one step behind him as they entered the final lap. With a burst of energy, the American attempted to speed around the Finn, only to have the Finn swerve to block him. The American made a second attempt in the opposite direction, again with the Finn blocking his path. The crowd broke into loud boos as the Finn won the race.

Being puzzled by such a response, the Finn was told of his conduct. Unaware of what he had done out of sheer exhaustion, the Finn not only apologized, but tried to refuse the gold medal. He was awarded the medal nonetheless. During the ceremony, he tried to pull the American up to the highest platform with him. The American graciously refused and the two men became lifelong friends. No formal protest was ever filed.

The Unattainable

"Do not be content with what you are able to do. Strive to achieve what you are able to do, and, if possible, the unattainable ....At the conclusion of the Games, go forth again to all quarters of the earth as heralds serving the good."

— Sven Hedin (Swedish explorer)
addressing the Olympic athletes
and spectators at the 1936 Berlin Games

No Quitter

During one of the final high-school meets of the year, Lee Calhoun knocked over one of the hurdles near the beginning of the race — a first for the season. This allowed the pack a considerable lead, but Lee managed to finish fifth, which gave his school the championship.

After the race, he was offered a scholarship to North Carolina Central University, his only college offer. Knowing he had not given his best performance, he questioned the recuiter. The reply, "Because of the determination I saw in you. You are not the type of person who would quit,...and that's the kind of person I want."

Calhoun went on to win gold medals in the hurdles at both the 1956 and 1960 Games.

"Identity"

Am I different? Possibly so
But only by searching do I ever know
The pain and the suffering of that pursuit
Emanate from the basic root
Of all mankind and his consuming goal
To keep immortal his fragile soul.[4]

— Donald Bragg, Pole Vault
Gold Medal, 1960 Rome Games

Getting Back Up

"If you have a meteoric rise, you inevitably have a meteoric fall. To me, that is the shooting star syndrome. We have seen many swimmers fall into that trap. You have to know how you did it. You have to know how you got there because inevitably you are going to trip over your shoe laces. When you trip over your shoe lace, it's all over unless you know how to get up and dust yourself off."

— Duncan Goodhew, Gold Medalist

One's Own Merits

"No one makes money from the Olympic Games. No one can buy an Olympic medal. There is no injustice of caste, of wealth, of family, of race. On the sports field everyone stands or falls on his own merits. The great lessons of the Olympic movement are here for all to see."

— Avery Brundage, President of IOC
1964 Tokyo Games
Spoken in both English and Japanese

First Big Win

*M*ike Larrabee, a high school math teacher, was nearly 31 when he went to the 1964 Games in Tokyo. A runner for 16 years, he had never won an important race. Although he was considered "ancient" as a runner — he snatched the victory in the 400-meter race from a field of much younger men, with a time of 45.1 seconds, the second fastest in Olympic history.

No Losers

"We simply put too much emphasis on always winning. Everyone who knows about my 1986 trip to Japan to race Osaki [whom he beat in the 1960 Games in Rome] always asks if I won again. I lost, but I didn't really lose. I swam faster at age 46 than I did the first time I placed in the nationals when I was 19. That's not losing. Someone just swam faster than I did."

— William Mulliken, Gold Medalist,
1960 Rome Games

Unusual Training

*D*ecathlon medalist Bruce Jenner trained for his event in a very unusual way. He made the equipment of the ten sports comprising the decathlon a part of his everyday life by filling his apartment with the "tools of the trade," where he would encounter them constantly during non-training hours. For example, believing the high hurdle was his weakest event, he placed a hurdle in the middle of his living room where he would have to step over it 25 or 30 times a day. An iron shot served as a doorstop. Instead of a charcoal grill on the terrace, Jenner had his barbells. The vaulting poles and javelins were stored behind the couch. The closets were full of sweat suits and running shoes. He said this type of exercise — both mental and physical — helped him improve his form as he prepared for the 1976 Games.

Finding Your Sport

Dr. Samuel Lee won gold and bronze medals for diving in the 1948 London and 1952 Helsinki Games — after earning a medical degree. He explained how he came to be a diver.

"My father emigrated from Korea to California in 1905....He originally planned to return to his homeland, but after the Japanese invaded Korea in 1910, he decided to stay, so he sent for my mother. They wanted their children to be born as free Americans.

"...When my father told me what the Olympics were all about, I told him that I wanted to be an Olympic champion. He laughed and asked, 'Well, in what sport?' I told him, 'Gee, I don't know, Pop, but some day I'll find it.' It was a lucky thing that no one threw me a basketball!"[5]

From Tears to Gold

Olga Korbut was the first internationally famous gymnast, and became the catalyst for the growth of women's gymnastics, as well as an inspiration to millions of aspiring gymnasts. However, many may have forgotten that her fame grew out of tremendous disappointment.

At Munich in 1972, Korbut lost her concentration on the asymmetrical bars and scored only 7.5 out of 10 — her lowest mark had been 9.4. Her ensuing tears, captured by close-up television cameras, tugged at the hearts of millions of viewers. Her subsequent return to win gold medals on the beam and in the floor exercise (as well as team gold) made her one of the greatest comeback athletes of all time. As she flashed her sparkling smile in victory, nearly all forgot her earlier devastation.

Believing You Are the Best

"The difference between winning and losing was simply belief. You have to be able to get up on the block and say to yourself, 'I am the best in the world!' You have to believe it one hundred percent. To break a world record, you have to say, 'Not only am I the best in the world, but I may be the very best that has ever been! In fact, I may be the best that will ever live!' Now to get your teeth onto that kind of thinking is very difficult to do. In fact, it is near impossible. Very few people can do it."

— Duncan Goodhew, Gold Medalist

OLYMPIC FACT:

The marathon, first staged in 1896, was a distance of 26 miles or 41.84 kilometers, the distance from the battlefield at Marathon to Athens. The modern marathon was extended to 42.195 km in 1908. It was run from Windsor to London, and the extra distance was added so that the race would start under the windows of the royal nursery at Windsor Castle. The distance was accepted as standard after a ruling in 1924.

To Throw It or Not?

*A*s captain of the Princeton track team, Bob Garrett was primarily a shot-putter, although he also competed in jumping events. When he decided to compete in the first modern Olympics in 1896, a professor suggested he also try throwing the discus. However, Princeton didn't even have a discus, neither did any other school they contacted.

The professor and Garrett consulted classical authorities to develop a design for a discus. Garrett took the drawings to a blacksmith who made a discus which weighed nearly 30 pounds! It was impossible to throw any distance, so he gave up on the idea of competing in the event.

Garrett paid his own way to the Olympics in Athens. Upon arriving, he discovered a "real" discus weighed less than five pounds. He began practicing immediately and decided to enter the event. On his third and final throw at the Games, Garrett beat the local favorite, Paraskevopoulos. He also won the shot-put and finished second in both the long jump and high jump.

In the 1900 Paris Games, Garrett placed third in the shot-put and standing triple jump, but didn't participate in the discus. His reason? His religious beliefs prohibited competing on Sunday.■

Winning in the Shadows

Julianne McNamara was the first American woman ever to win an individual gold medal on the parallel bars, achieving her victory with daring moves attempted by very few women. That fact, however, was hardly noticed because the limelight at the 1984 Games was on her teammate, Mary Lou Retton. Few also noticed that McNamara won a silver medal in the floor exercise, ahead of Retton who won the bronze. Together, she and Retton led the U.S. gymnasts to a team silver medal.

McNamara once said, "I'm striving for a 10 every time out," and she did achieve five perfect scores of 10 during the Olympics, a record for an American gymnast — but also a fact that went virtually unheralded. While much of the attention was focused elsewhere, McNamara just kept on winning!

Going All Out

"*P*art way through the competition I was thinking that I was diving well, and it was kind of scary. You have to have just enough of a distraction so you can concentrate on what you want to be doing. You can say to yourself, 'Don't mess up.' Many times you get stuck in that and that's when you start holding back. I didn't want to do that today. I wanted to go all out."

— Greg Louganis, Diving Gold Medalist

Training Retreat

A year-and-a-half before the 1984 Olympic Games, 15 members and 3 coaches of the U.S. men's volleyball team went on a retreat. The squad spent three frigid January weeks traversing 80 rugged miles of Canyonlands National Park in southern Utah — much of it in snowshoes. It was part of an outdoor survival course designed to test the mettle of individuals tough enough to take on an Olympic challenge.

Assistant Coach Bill Neville said, "In order to complete our total training program...and to provide the most positive and influential experience, we wanted to involve the team in a wilderness situation that would uniquely tap the human resources required in every stress situation. We wanted our players to be totally prepared when they marched into the Olympic Stadium in 1984 to represent the United States."

The Struggle

"*T*he most important thing in the Olympic Games is not to win but to take part, just as the most important thing in life is not the triumph but the struggle."

— Baron Pierre de Coubertin

Overcoming All Odds

*W*ilma Rudolph grew up in a large, poor, black family, one of the youngest of twenty children. She understood severe racial prejudice, and was also attacked by illness — including double pneumonia and scarlet fever. At age six, polio paralyzed her right leg. Members of her family massaged her leg four times a day. Finally, at age eight, she began walking with a brace. At twelve, she walked with corrective shoes. When shoes seemed unwieldy, she would play barefoot.

Then Wilma decided to try running. At age 15, she was winning state competitions, and at 16, made her Olympic debut, winning a bronze medal. At the Rome Olympics in 1960, at the age of 20, she won triple gold — including the prestigious 10-meters title. She won the 100-meter dash by *three* meters and the 200-meter dash by *four* meters!

Triumph Against the Odds

"*I* had to be fast, otherwise there was nothing left to eat on the table."

— Wilma Rudolph

The Smarter Option

"*W*hen I used to come home all beat up...my father would say, 'Boy, you either have to learn how to fight or how to run. It's as simple as that.' So I learned to run. I thought running was the smarter thing to do."

— Raymond Barbuti, Runner
2 Gold Medals, 1928 Amsterdam Games

Decathlon Celebration

*A*fter he became the youngest person ever to win a gold medal in the decathlon at the 1948 Olympics, Bob Mathias was asked how he intended to celebrate. The 17-year-old quipped, "I'll start shaving, I guess."

Lessons from Sports

"We all have dreams. But in order to make these dreams into reality it takes an awful lot of determination, self-discipline, and effort. Sports teaches those things and others — respect of other people, and how to live with your fellow man."

— Jesse Owens, Gold Medal Runner
1936 Berlin Games

A Friend at the Line

*F*ew doubted that world record holder Jesse Owens would win the long jump at the 1936 Berlin Games. However, on his first qualifying jump he launched beyond the regulation line. His second attempt was identical.

At that point Luz Long, a tall, blue-eyed, blond German athlete introduced himself to Owens and said, "You should be able to qualify with your eyes closed!" He then suggested that since the qualifying distance was only 23 feet, 5-1/2 inches, he should make a mark several inches before the takeoff board and jump from there to play it safe. Owens followed the advice and qualified easily. When Owens set the Olympic record in the finals, Long was the first to congratulate him in full view of Hitler.

Owens later wrote, "You could melt down all the medals and cups I have, but they wouldn't be a plating on the 24-carat friendship I felt for Luz Long."

A Terrific Experience

"My sports have been terrific to me. I've gone all over the world — places I'd never have got to except for competing. I've made good friends, and traveling and meeting people helped me develop my personality. When I was a kid I was sort of introverted. I'm not any more. Sure, I've paid the price — you have to do that to get to the top. But it was worth it. I wouldn't trade places with anybody."

— Sheila Young, Gold Medalist

Gallantry on the Seas

*D*uring the fifth day of sailing competition during the 1988 Seoul Games, winds were raging at 35 knots and the swells were at 15 feet when two sailors on the Singapore team were thrown overboard as their boat capsized.

Canada's Lawrence Lemieux, sailing alone in a different heat, saw the sailors in distress. He rescued one of them, who had become exhausted from struggling against the strong currents, but the diversion caused him to fall well behind in his own race.

Judges awarded Lemieux second place in the heat, the position he was in when he went to the sailors' aid. Although he didn't win a medal, the IOC gave him a special award for his gallantry. Lemieux downplayed the attention saying simply, "It's the first rule of sailing to help people in distress."

Young Victor

*B*etty Robinson was the first American woman to win a gold medal in track and field with her 1928 win in the 100-meter race. At the same Games, she also won a silver in the 400-meter relay. Her accomplishments were all the more remarkable because she was only 16 at the time, and the Olympics was only the fourth time she had run in a formal track meet!

Over the next two-and-a-half years Robinson set four world records — the 100-meter, 100-yard, 70-yard, and 60-yard dashes. Soon after she was in a plane crash and suffered a severely broken leg, a crushed arm, and a serious concussion which put her in a coma for nearly two months. After a slow and painful recovery, she returned to the Olympics in 1936. Because of her injuries she used a standing start, and still won her second gold medal!

OLYMPIC FACT:

As of January 4, 1996, the Atlanta Games had an historic 100 percent turnout. All 197 nations invited by the International Olympic Committee to compete in Atlanta agreed to take part. This marked the first time in the post-war era that all nations affiliated with the IOC agreed to compete. It also set a record for number of nations involved — the previous record of 169 nations was set at the 1992 Games in Barcelona.

No Sloppy Workouts

"The champion athlete does not simply do more of the same drills and sets as other swimmers; he or she also does things better. That's what counts. Very small differences, consistently practiced, will produce results. In swimming it could be doing all turns legally, or swimming one extra set of repeats after practice every day, or wearing gloves on your hands to keep them warm at a meet.

"The results of such quality training inevitably add up. Swimming is swimming, we can say — in practice, or in meets, it's all the same. If you swim sloppily for 364 days a year, nothing great is going to happen on the day of that one big meet, no matter how excited you get."[6]

— Daniel F. Chambliss, coach

Relaxation

"*W*hatever success I have had is due to being so perfectly relaxed that I can feel my jaw muscles wiggle."

—Bobby Joe Morrow, Gold Medal Runner
1956 Melbourne Games

Continual Record-Breaking

*I*t has been said that Johnny Weissmuller was such a fine swimmer he had very little real competition in the Olympics. In the 1924 Games he won the 100-meter and 400-meter freestyle events, anchored the team that set a world record in the 200-meter freestyle relay, and helped the U.S. water polo team win a bronze medal. He returned to the 1928 Olympics in Paris to win the 100-meter freestyle event and to anchor the winning relay team. In all, he set 24 world records in 10 years of swimming.

Weissmuller seemed to have an uncanny knack for being able to control his pace with precision. When Johnny went on exhibition tours, it was said that his coach advised him not to break any record by too wide a margin — rather, to shave off just a fraction of a second from his previous world record. That way, when he went to the next exhibition town he could thrill the crowd there with a new record-breaking swim!

OLYMPIC FACT:

Swimmer Johnny
Weissmuller starred in
the first of 12 Tarzan
movies in 1932.
He later said about that
role, "It was up my alley.
There was swimming
in it, and I didn't
have much to say."

Fast or Slow?

*E*mil Zatopek of Czechoslovakia was an athlete who seemed "bigger than life." Bursting with enthusiasm, he was known for his honesty, charm, humility, and his great courage in the face of government repression. Part of his legend stems from his distinctive running style — head cocked, arms flailing, and face contorted in pain. He was nicknamed, "The Human Locomotive."

After winning several gold medals in the 1952 Games, he surprised his countrymen by declaring he would run the marathon, a race he had never attempted, even in training. Because of his running style many thought he would never finish the race. But he not only finished six minutes faster than the Olympic record, he stood calmly munching an apple as the second-place runner crossed the finish line. Track attendants reported Zatopek wasn't even out of breath when he finished the race!

Fast!

"Why should I practice running slow? I already know how to run slow. I want to learn how to run fast!"

—Emil Zatopek

Crossing the Fine Line

"'There is a fine line between being a good gymnast and being a champion,' [Coach] Mako said. 'You just decide how badly you want to cross that line.' I trusted him, and he was right. In fact, after that week [of initial intense training] was finally over, I realized I had never felt such satisfaction. Not because I won anything, because I hadn't, but because I had done it. I had done what I set out to do, and because of that, I felt like a champion.

"Now here it was, the Olympics. We had achieved the impossible. We had won the gold. Some people may think it ludicrous that in the heat of the excitement and the thrill of that moment, I was thinking only of such a seemingly insignificant time as that one week of training. But it was because of that week that my commitment had been solidified, and I had proved to myself I could do it. As I stood on the winner's stand, the real meaning behind that week became clear — it was not the repetition of the routines that had been important, but the strengthening of my mind, the reinforcement that I could reach my dream."[7]

— Timothy Daggett, Gymnast
and Gold Medalist

Been There Before

"Just before the green light went on for my turn, I looked at my coach, Makot Sakamoto, the man with whom I had been working for twelve long years. I gave him a smile, and he smiled back and said, 'OK, let's go. Just like in the gym. You've done this a thousand times.' That's when it hit me. *Of course, I'm prepared. I've done this every day at the end of my workouts.*

"In practice, I had always tried to imagine myself in competition, and now it was the other way around. I was mentally trying to take myself out of Pauley Pavilion and its 10,000 noisy fans and back into the UCLA gym with two or three people watching. It worked. When I grabbed the bar, I really felt like I was home. I did my routine and scored a 9.95. Now there was no doubt. We had won the team gold."[8]

— Peter Vidmar, Gymnast, 2 Gold Medals,
1 Silver Medal, 1984 Los Angeles Games

Steel and Softness

*T*he question was asked by a journalist, "What does it take to be an Olympic gymnast?"

"Guts and nerves of steel — and a touch of softness."

> — Kathy Johnson, Gymnast
> Silver Medalist
> 1984 Los Angeles Games

Regrouping

"There's no other feeling like winning the Olympic Games. You stand on the podium and know that you are the best in the world, but you also know that you may never be there again. The hardest thing after you've won an Olympic medal is to regroup and start over again [in training]."

— Darrell Pace, Gold Medal Archer
1976 Montreal and 1984 Los Angeles Games

True "Ice"

In sports, the term "ice" is often used for an athlete who displays extraordinary inner control. One such Olympian was Shun Fujimoto, a Japanese gymnast in the 1976 Games. He broke his leg during his first event, the floor exercises, but went on to perform on the pommel horse and then on the rings. His demanding routine of skill and strength on the rings represented graceful poise in the context of intense personal pain and public pressure. His superb performance, including a successful dismount on his broken leg, assured the Japanese gymnastic team a gold medal in that Olympics. Fujimoto was a true "ice man."

Olympic Motto

*T*he English version of the Olympic motto translates:

    Swifter, Higher, Stronger

The original motto was written in Latin: *Citius, Altius, Fortius,* and was adopted at the 1920 Antwerp Games.

OLYMPIC FACTS:

One of the shortest male champions at the Games was bantamweight Joe de Pietro, who stood only 4 foot 6 inches.

Artur von Pongracz was 72-years-old when he made the Austrian equestrian team.

The youngest champion ever crowned was 12-year-old Aileen Riggin, who won the springboard diving event for the United States in the 1920 Antwerp Games.

The Outer Limits

*A*fter satisfying himself that there must be some absolute limits to human strength, speed, agility, and endurance, Brutus Hamilton, coach of the U.S. Olympic team some twenty years ago, compiled a list of what he considered to be the "ultimate" in track and field performance. Based on his long experience in coaching, Hamilton said that no one would ever...

- run the 100-yard dash in less than 9.2 seconds,
- run the mile in less than 3 minutes, 57.8 seconds,
- put the shot more than 62 feet,
- throw the discus more than 200 feet,
- pole vault higher than 16 feet, or
- complete a high jump better than 7 feet, 1 inch.

Since his prediction, every one of these records has been broken.

OLYMPIC FACT:

Until Alvin Kraenzlein, hurdlers simply jumped over the hurdles as well as they could. It was Kraenzlein who developed the modern technique of going over the hurdle with a straight front leg and the trailing leg tucked under.

Kraenzlein is the only athlete ever to win four individual track and field gold medals at a single Olympics (1900) — the 60-meter dash, the 110-meter hurdles, the 220-meter hurdles, and the long jump.

Give Away

*E*very time Olympic medalist Gary Hall took an overseas trip, he took along an extra trunk — with his coach's and the officials' permission. This extra trunk was filled with shirts and Levi's and other items of clothing that Hall proceeded to give away. He always took the "in thing" that was in style, and he always took new clothes. He never traded them — he gave them away to other competing athletes. His coach recalls that he "never had even his own sweats by the time he returned home."

The Way It Should Be

"You come over here, and it's the Olympics. You say it's the field of battle, and you're here for a gold medal. You're with people who eat sport, drink sport, make a living from sport. Then something like this happens, and all these people, the whole Olympic Village, the whole community, together, are asking to help. Everyone. You talk about the Olympic spirit, well, this is more than you ever dreamt was possible. This is the way life should be."[9]

— Ron Karnaugh, 1992 Barcelona Games
(Father died at opening ceremonies)

Last, But Not Sad

A construction worker, Pyambuu Tuul had lost his vision in an explosion in his hometown in 1978. After two unsuccessful operations, he had little hope of seeing again. Then the New York Achilles Track Club, which promotes athletics for the disabled, invited him to the 1990 New York Marathon. Led by a guide, he walked most of the way. The club later arranged for a cornea transplant for Tuul, which was performed in January 1991.

At the 1992 Barcelona Games, he was the first Mongolian to run the marathon — and the last runner to finish. But this gave him distinction. He was the "last competitor" of the 1992 Olympics!

OLYMPIC FACT:

Janice Lee York was a member of six Olympic fencing teams from 1948 to 1968 and was the first woman to carry the American flag at the opening ceremonies (1968).

After the Gold

"It was four years of being scolded for making the same mistakes. I enjoyed it at the time, but I was quite ready to leave it once the four years were over....

"When competing was over, I got out of it and went on to the next thing in my life — to study medicine and become a doctor.

"That's what sports did for me above anything else. They taught me to set goals for myself and then to go out and pursue them."[10]

— Benjamin Spock, M.D.

Champions of Inspiration
(1984 Games)

• Greg Barton was born with club feet and underwent four major surgeries. He won the bronze medal in men's kayaking.

• Jim Martinson, once a downhill racer, lost both legs in a land-mine explosion in Vietnam. He competed in the wheelchair race, one of the events offered for the first time for the physically disabled.

• Nelson Vails spent most of his life in the slums of Harlem and became aware of his biking talents as he delivered messages on the streets of Manhattan to earn a living. He is one of few black cyclists who cycled his way to a silver medal.

Bridging Differences

*M*ary Peters was born in England but she lived most of her life in Belfast, Northern Ireland. As a young athlete, she struggled against a lack of money and facilities. She was a virtual "unknown" in the sports world.

Mary competed in the pentathlon in 1964 and again in Mexico in 1968, but took home no medals. She was popular with other team members, the public, and even her rivals. At Munich in 1972, Mary took the lead and won the gold! At age 33, she reached the top of her athletic career.

Mary returned to Belfast and raised funds to build the first international running track in Northern Ireland.

Nervous No More

*A*rcher Darrell Pace was only 15 years old when he first tried out for an Olympic team. He was so nervous his first two arrows missed the target completely! He lacked 10 points from qualifying for the U.S. team, equal to one bull's eye.

After that, however, Pace earned a spot on nine World Target Championship teams and four Olympic teams. In the 1976 Olympics, he set a world record of 2,571 points and won the gold medal. In 1984, he won his second individual gold medal and in 1988, won a silver medal in team competition.

Coach's Challenge

"Swear that you'll work a year with me without question and I'll take you on. You won't swim against anybody. You'll just be a slave and you'll hate my guts, but in the end you just might break every record there is."

— Bill Bachrach, coach to Johnny Weissmuller

Inside Desire

"*I*'m a great believer that you can't make anyone a champion unless they want to be a champion. You can't make someone something without it being inside of them to start with."

— Sharon Davies, Swimming
Silver Medal, 1980 Moscow Games

Single-Handed!

*P*itcher Jim Abbott is one of the most remarkable athletes ever to put on a uniform. Born without a right hand, he learned early in life to adapt when playing sports, especially baseball, the game he dearly loved.

Jim was selected to pitch for the United States at the 1988 Olympics in Seoul. The starting pitcher for the final game with Japan, he pitched a full nine innings, gave up only seven hits, and shut down a rally in the eighth inning with a fine fielding play. He retired 11 of the last 12 batters, helping the United States defeat Japan 5-3 for the gold!

Only His Left

*W*hile working as a butcher's apprentice, Joe Frazier was called to join the U.S. boxing team for the 1964 Tokyo Games. He had lost in the trials to Buster Mathis, but when Mathis broke a knuckle, Joe had his chance.

In his semifinal match, Frazier knocked his opponent to the canvas twice with punches so powerful the opponent's trainers signaled to stop the fight. In the match for the gold medal, Joe only used his left hand, to the dismay of his trainers. He still won the fight, however, by a close decision. The next day, Frazier not only wore his gold medal proudly around his neck, but a cast on his right hand. He had broken it during his semifinal match, but didn't tell anyone lest he be eliminated from the finals. By 1970, Joe had become the heavy-weight champion of the world!

Performance Tells the Story

In 1968 swimmer Mark Spitz brashly predicted that he would win four, five, maybe six gold medals at the Summer Games in Mexico City. Instead, he won only one bronze, one silver, and two golds in relay events. In the 200-meter butterfly, in which he held the world record, he finished last, almost five body lengths behind the winner.

Four years later he made no predictions, but let his swimming tell the story. This time he won the 200-meter butterfly by two body lengths and set a world record. He also set world records and won gold medals in six other events: 200-meter freestyle, 100-meter butterfly, 100-meter freestyle relay, 200-meter freestyle relay, and 100-meter medley relay — for a total of seven gold medals and seven world records! He was the first swimmer to win more than five gold medals in an Olympiad.

How Far?

*B*ob Beamon prepared for the '68 Olympics without a coach. When finals began, he sprinted down the runway, hit the takeoff board, and launched himself about five-and-a-half feet into the air for what seemed a very long distance. The judges announced the jump had measured 8.90 meters. Bob didn't know what that meant until Boston told him he had jumped 29 feet, 2-1/2 inches — a world record that stood for 23 years!

One of his competitors withdrew saying, "I can't go on. We'll all look silly."

Retraining

*K*aroly Takacs of Hungary won the world championship in pistol shooting in 1937 and was favored to win a gold medal at the 1940 Olympics. Then in 1938, as a sergeant in the Hungarian army, a grenade exploded in his right hand — his shooting hand — destroying it completely. No one thought he would ever shoot again.

World War II broke out in 1939 and both the 1940 and 1944 Games were canceled because of it. In 1948 the Olympics resumed, held in London. Takacs entered the pistol-shooting competition, stepped to the line, and drew his pistol to shoot — this time using his left hand. He had taught himself to shoot all over again. By then he was 38 years old. He scored 580 points in the competition and won the gold medal by a large margin. He repeated his gold-medal victory at the 1952 Games in Helsinki.

Team Spirit

*"T*he team got together so well. We had so much spirit that it's really hard to describe. Everybody was rooting for each other. There were no cliques and no animosity between swimmers. We were all out to prove one thing. We were out to prove that we were the best."

— Kathy Heddy-Silver, Swimming
1976 Montreal Games

Even in Pain

*A*fter suffering a crushing loss in 1977, Japanese judo player Yasuhiro Yamashita vowed he would never lose again. For the next seven years, he won 194 matches and lost none. He was held to a draw only once in 1980, when an opponent fell on his ankle and broke it. He won all but five of his matches by *ippon*, equivalent to a pin in wrestling.

In the second match of the 1984 Los Angeles Games, Yamashita tore a muscle in his right calf. He won the match, but was in great pain when he tried to put weight on his leg. His next opponent attacked the injured leg, but Yamashita quickly recovered and ended the match seconds later. In the final, Yamashita's opponent again attacked his injured leg, but he counterattacked and scored *ippon* only one minute and five seconds after the match started. Afterward, he was in such pain his opponent kindly helped him onto the awards platform to receive his gold medal.

The Measure of Victory

"I found it very difficult to smile when my performance didn't live up to my expectations. By not breaking the world record I felt I had not only let myself down, but also the crowd."

— Richard "Rick" Carey, Gold Medalist,
Swimmer, 1984 Olympics

Personal victory is best measured by those who have achieved it.

Stamina

"*S*tamina isn't just a question of a strong heart, lungs like a pair of bellows, and elastic muscles. More important is your mental attitude."

— Fanny Blankers-Koen,
  Netherlands Gold Medalist
  1948 London Games

Even with Paralysis

*I*n 1944, Lis Hartel was one of the top dressage competitors in Denmark. Then she was stricken with polio and in a matter of days her body was almost totally paralyzed. Lis worked hard to overcome her paralysis — after a few months she was able to crawl, and in less than a year she could walk with crutches. She was determined to ride again, but first she had to relearn the use of all the muscles that held her on a horse. Her first riding attempt exhausted her so much she had to rest two full weeks before trying again.

Five years later she represented Denmark at the 1952 Helsinki Games, the first time women were allowed to compete in dressage alongside men. Lis was still paralyzed below the knees and had to be helped on and off her horse, but she and her horse Jubilee won the silver medal.

Only Winning

"*I* am not concerned about records — only winning. So many men have lost races worrying about the time or opposition. In the Olympic Games you can never be sure who is the most dangerous rival and therefore it is better to concentrate on your own performance. Even if you break a world record it does not last, but you can never take away an Olympic title."

— Murray Halberg , Runner
Gold Medalist, 1960 Rome Games

The Superior Festival

*W*ater is most excellent of earthly things.

Of splendid wealth, gold shines brightest,
like fire glowing in darkness.

O my soul, shall we sing of crowns and contests?
Then know this —

The sun warms more than any lesser star,
and no festival outshines Olympia.

— opening lines of *Olympian Ode* I by Pindar

Value in Competition

"*P*eace could be furthered by the Olympic Games...peace could be the product only of a better world; a better world could be brought about only by better individuals; and better individuals could be developed only by the give and take, the buffeting and battering, the stress and strain of fierce competition."

— Baron Pierre de Coubertin
Founder of the modern Olympic Games

A Thousand Little Decisions

"*G*reat accomplishments, we often assume, require heroic motivation: an intense desire to be the best, an inner strength beyond all measure, some special love of school, of family, of country. Some one of these must, we think, drive the superlative athlete....

"In fact, world-class athletes get to the top level by making a thousand little decisions every morning and night. If you make the right choice on each of these — decide to get up and go to practice, decide to work hard today, decide to volunteer to do an extra event to help your team — then others will say you 'have' dedication. But it is only the doing of those little things, all taken together, that makes that dedication. Great [athletes] aren't made in the long run; they are made every day."[11]

— Daniel F. Chambliss, coach

You Must Run This Race Alone

*W*hen Fred Newhouse failed to make the 1972 U.S. Olympic team, he poured his energies into earning an MBA. But with his wife's encouragement, he began training for the 1976 Games. He battled discouragement, as he had no one with whom to train and since he was out of college few qualifying races were open to him.

Newhouse gained inspiration during his darkest hour when he viewed a documentary on Ethiopian marathon runner Abebe Bikila entitled "You Must Run This Race Alone." Fred took the title of the program as his personal motto, and went on to win both gold and silver medals in the 1976 Games.

An Unusual Autograph

*A*fter the 100-meter relay race at the 1960 Olympics, during which Wilma Rudolph had run her leg of the race faster than any woman had ever run, she was surrounded by a large crowd of those who sought autographs and photographs. Finally, only one fan remained — a young boy. He shyly asked Wilma for her autograph and handed her a pen and piece of paper. Wilma, however, went a step beyond. She untied her running shoes, signed her name on each of them, and gave them to him.

OLYMPIC FACT:

American James Connolly won the triple jump with a leap of 44 feet, 11-3/4 inches, and became the first Olympic victor of modern times (1896). His record was inscribed on a special board and the American flag was hoisted on a high pole before the entrance of the stadium in Athens.

To the Finish

*I*n a semifinal race at the 1992 Barcelona Games, Derek Redmond of Great Britain went down on the backstretch with a torn right hamstring. As medical attendants approached him, Redmond fought to his feet. As if from an "animal instinct" he set out hopping toward the finish line in a crazed attempt to finish the race. As he reached the stretch, a large man in a T-shirt rushed out of the stands, hurled aside a security guard, and ran onto the track. It was Jim Redmond, Derek's father. "You don't have to do this," he told his weeping son. "Yes, I do," replied Derek. "Well, then," said Jim, "we're going to finish this together." With Derek's head at times buried in his father's shoulder, the two stayed in the lane to the end. The watching crowd arose in a massive ovation and wept with them as Derek finished his race.

The Comeback Trail

When Pablo Morales went to the 1984 Games in Los Angeles, he was the best butterfly swimmer in the world and expected to win the 100-meter race. But when he looked at the scoreboard after his swim, he was disappointed to find he was second. In 1988, he failed to make the Olympic team, so he turned to other pursuits. Later he decided to try a comeback. At the time his mother was dying of cancer and he had only seven months before the Olympic trials to train.

He finally realized his dream in the 1992 Games at the age of 27.

Emotional Ending

"*I* just swam to the end and waited. I didn't want to get too emotional. I turned around and looked. Once something like this happens, you wonder if it really happened. You wonder the same way if you win or if you lose. Did it really happen?"[12]

— Pablo Morales, Gold Medal Swimmer,
1992 Barcelona Games

The 47-Second Barrier

*I*n the world of 400-meter hurdlers, the 47-second barrier had stood for nine years (Edwin Moses' world record 47.02). Going into the 1992 Barcelona Games, Kevin Young was determined to break this barrier. He wrote on the wall in his Olympic Village room: "46.89."

As the race unfolded, Young was ten meters ahead of the field, sailing smoothly, without a break in stride over the first twelve hurdles. All that stood between him and a gold medal was the final hurdle. Then his heel hit the top of the last hurdle and drove the barrier down. Young thought of nothing but keeping his balance. He kept moving, his momentum intact, and drove on. As he looked to the board for his time, he was elated to find 46.78 appear in lights. A new world record by .24 seconds!

All-Round Victory

*J*ackie Joyner-Kersee, considered one of the most outstanding track and field athletes in history, became the first American woman to set a world record in an Olympic multi-event competition. She won a silver medal in the 1984 heptathlon, then went on to earn a record 7,148 points in the 1986 Goodwill Games in Moscow for the heptathlon. She won gold medals in both the 1988 and 1992 Olympics, setting a world record long-jump in 1988. When she repeated her heptathlon win in the 1992 Barcelona Games, she became the first athlete of either gender to win multi-event medals in three Olympics.

Few know she had to overcome asthma to accomplish such feats. Her victory over disease is just as impressive as her victories in track and field!

OLYMPIC FACT:

In 1896, only 311 athletes competed in the first Games of the modern Olympiad. By contrast, 9,581 athletes competed in the 1992 Summer Olympics in Barcelona.

Avoiding the Psych-Out

"The psyching process is a very strange thing. We talk about it and yet we don't really understand it. You could say to so and so, 'I'm going to beat you!' Most good swimmers would take that in and say, 'No way! No you are not!' A lesser swimmer would think that maybe they were indeed going to be beaten. They'll be thinking, 'Can he beat me? Is he going to beat me?' It's that question of doubt and that is where you can get psyched out."

— David Wilkie, Great Britain
1976 Gold Medalist

Fencing Fame

*E*doardo Mangiarotti started out to be a right-hander. His father, already having one son who showed skills to make him a World Champion, changed Edoardo to a left-handed fencer, however, in order that Edoardo might be the best ever *left-handed* fencer in the world. His ploy worked. Mangiarotti began winning world titles in 1937 and continued to be a member of winning teams until the 1960 Games.

In all, he won 6 gold, 5 silver, and 2 bronze medals in individual and team fencing events.

Two Hundred Proposals

*L*ess than two months after his coach suggested he try the decathlon, Bob Mathias not only qualified for the U.S. Olympic track team, but went on to win the competition. When Mathias returned, his plane had to circle until the runway was cleared of the many admirers awaiting him. He was awarded the Sullivan Award as the nation's outstanding amateur athlete and he received more than 200 marriage proposals!

Four years later, Mathias easily won the gold medal again, setting a world record of 7,887 points, a 900 point margin of victory over his closest competitor and the largest lead in Olympic decathlon history. He was the only athlete to ever win the Olympic decathlon twice.

Mathias later served as a U.S. congressman and was director of the Olympic Training Center in Colorado Springs.

A Different Motivation

General Sir Philip Christison was confident that the sound of pipes and drums would spur his running Scot, 22-year-old Eric Liddell. But in the end, it was something quite different which motivated Liddell when it came time to run in the 1924 Paris Games.

A masseur officially assigned to care for the British team had come to know Eric quite well in the days leading up to his races. He intuitively sensed that this man's spirit was different. When Eric refused to run the 100-meter race because it was held on Sunday, the masseur clearly knew what was in Liddell's heart.

When a fellow athlete withdrew from the 400-meter contest on a following weekday, Liddell requested to take his place, even though he had not trained for the event.

As Liddell left his hotel for the Colombes Stadium where he was to attempt to run the 400, the masseur handed him a piece of folded paper. Eric glanced at it and said, "Thank you. I'll read it when I get to the stadium." In a quiet moment later that day, he opened the paper to read: "In the old book it says, 'He that honors me I will honor.' Wishing you the best of success always."

When Liddell crossed the finish line in first place he was no longer a traitor for not running on Sunday, but a national hero. He viewed this change of the public's heart with part amusement, part disinterest. His motivation lay elsewhere.■

Endnotes

[1]Duff Hart-Davis, *Tales of Gold*, (New York: Contemporary Books, 1987), 447.

[2]Ibid., 435-436.

[3]Rick Ortiz, *Legacies*, (Newport Beach, CA: Metro Lifestyles and Design, 1992), 36.

[4]Hart-Davis, *Tales of Gold*, 299.

[5]Ibid., 231.

[6]Daniel F. Chambliss, *The Making of Olympic Swimmers*, (New York: Morrow and Company, 1988), 213-214.

[7]Tim Daggett, *Dare to Dream*, (Tarrytown, NY: Wynwood, 1992), 17.

[8]Hart-Davis, *Tales of Gold*, 497.

[9]*Sports Illustrated*, August 10, 1992: p. 35.

[10]Larry Bortstein, *After Olympic Glory*, (New York: Frederick Warne, 1978), 151.

[11]Chambliss, *Olympic Swimmers*, 93-94.

[12]*Sports Illustrated*, April 3, 1992: p. 36-39.

Olympic Bibliography

Aaseng, Nate. *Great Summer Olympic Moments.* Minneapolis: Lerner Publications, 1990.

Benyo, Richard. *The Masters of the Marathon.* New York: Atheneum, 1983.

Blue, Adrianne. *Faster, Higher, Further.* London: Virago Press, 1988.

Bortstein, Larry. *After Olympic Glory* . New York: Frederick Warne, 1978.

Chambliss, Daniel F. *The Making of Olympic Swimmers.* New York: Morrow and Company, 1988.

Chester, David. *The Olympic Game Handbook.* New York: Charles Scribner's Sons, 1971.

Davis, Michael D. *Black American Women in Olympic Track and Field.* Jefferson, NC: McFarland, 1992.

Durant, John. *Highlights of the Olympics.* New York: Hastings House Publishers, 1969.

Daggett, Tim. *Dare to Dream.* Tarrytown, NY: Wynwood, 1992.

Finley, M.I. and H.W. Pleket. *The Olympic Games — The First Thousand Years.* New York: Viking, 1976.

Glubok, Shirley and Alfred Tamarin. *Olympic Games in Ancient Greece.* New York: Harper & Row, 1976.

Hart-Davis, Duff. *Tales of Gold.* New York: Contemporary Books, 1987.

Hickok, Ralph. *A Who's Who of Sports Champions.* New York: Houghton Mifflin, 1995.

Hugman, Barry, and Peter Arnold. *The Olympic Games.* New York: Facts on File, 1988.

Johnson, William Oscar. *The Olympics, A History of the Games.* Birmingham, AL: Oxmoor House, 1992.

Kent, Zachary. *U.S. Olympians*. Chicago: Children's Press, 1992.

Killanin, Lord, and John Rodda, eds. *The Olympic Games: 80 Years of People, Events and Records*. New York: Collier Books, 1976.

Killanin, Lord and John Rodda, eds. *The Olympic Games 1980*. New York: Macmillan, 1979.

Krise, Raymond, and Bill Squires. *Fast Tracks — the History of Distance Running*. Brattleboro, VT: The Stephen Greene Press, 1982.

Laklan, Carli. *Golden Girls*. New York: McGraw-Hill, 1980.

Litsky, Frank. *The Winter Olympics*. Franklin Watts — A First Book, 1979.

Mallay, Stephen. *The Kids' Guide to the 1992 Summer Olympics*. New York: Time, 1992

Merrison, Tim. *Field Athletics*. New York: Crestwood House, 1991.

Ortiz, Rick. *Legacies*. Newport Beach: Metro Lifestyles and Design, 1992.

Segrave, Jeffrey, and Donald Chu, eds. *Olympism*. Champaign, IL: Human Kinetics Publishers, 1981.

Sullivan, George. *Modern Olympic Superstars*. New York: Dodd, Mead & Company, 1979.

Swift, Catherine. *Eric Liddell*. Minneapolis: Bethany House, 1990.

Tan, Paul Lee, ed. *Encyclopedia of 7700 Illustrations*. Garland, TX: Bible Communications, 1969.

Tatlow, Peter. *The Olympics*. New York: Bookwright Press, 1987.

Toomey, Bill, and Barry King. *The Olympic Challenge*. Costa Mesa, CA: HDL Publishing, 1988.

U.S. Olympic Committee. *The Olympic Games*. Colorado Springs, CO: U.S. Olympic Committee, January 1983.

Wallechinsky, David. *The Complete Book of the Olympics*. New York: Penguin Books, 1984, 1988.

Additional copies of this book and other
Trade Life titles are available
at your local bookstore.

Now I Know Why Life Is Like An Olympic Dream
by The Rhymeo Brothers

*How To Be The Man Of Your Wife's Dreams
And Not Her Worst Nightmare*

*How To Be The Woman Of Your Husband's Dreams
And Not His Worst Nightmare*

Dittohead's Little Instruction Book

The Little Book of Business Etiquette
by Valerie Sokolosky

Trade Life
P.O. Box 55325
Tulsa, Oklahoma 74155